Forever MARILYN

Forever MARILYN

Marie Cahill

This edition published in 1992 by SMITHMARK Publishers Inc., 112 Madison Avenue New York, New York 10016

SMITHMARK books are available for bulk purchase for sales promotion and premium use. For details write or telephone the Manager of Special Sales, SMITHMARK Publishers Inc., 112 Madison Avenue, New York, NY 10016. (212) 532-6600.

Produced by Brompton Books Corp., 15 Sherwood Place Greenwich, CT 06830

ISBN 0-8317-3470-1

Printed in Hong Kong

10 9 8 7 6 5 4 3 2 1

CONTENTS

Introduction	6
Growing Up	8
Marilyn, the Model	11
The Road to Hollywood	12
Glamour Girl	15
Ingénue	16
The Asphalt Jungle	18
Hollywood Starlet	21
Sex Symbol	22
Gentlemen Prefer Blondes	25
Movie Star	27
On Hollywood's Roller Coaster	28
Marilyn and Joe	31
Entertaining the Troops	32
The Seven Year Itch	35
Marilyn–At Her Best	36
Egghead Weds Hourglass	38
The Prince and the Showgirl	41
The Many Faces of Marilyn	42
Some Like It Hot	46
Let's Make Love	49
Blonde Bombshell	50
The Misfits	53
The Tragic Decline of Marilyn	54
Something's Got to Give	57
Tributes to Marilyn	58
Marilyn Remembered	60
Index	64

Page 1: The alluring Marilyn as captured by photographer Philippe Halsman in 1959.
Pages 2-3: Marilyn Monroe, one of Hollywood's most luminous and unforgettable stars.
Pages 4-5: Marilyn Monroe, with Richard Widmark, in *Don't Bother to Knock*, 1952 (*left*) and *There's No Business Like Show Business*, 1954 (*right*).

Designed by Ruth DeJauregui

INTRODUCTION

On 1 June 1926, Gladys Pearl Baker Mortensen gave birth to her third child, a daughter whom she named Norma Jeane. Her first two children, a son and another daughter, were living in Kentucky with their father. Gladys had remarried, but Edward Mortensen, her second husband–like her first–had left her, and it is almost certain that Mortensen was not the father of Norma Jeane. In later years, Norma Jeane would discover a photo of a man who bore a striking resemblance to Clark Gable. Gladys told her daughter that the man in the photo–Stanley C Gifford–was her father. Gifford denied the child was his, and so little Norma Jeane grew up never knowing–but always seeking–her father.

The poor child was often without her mother, as well, for Gladys could not care for Norma Jeane and left her with foster parents. When Norma Jeane was about six, she and her mother did live together briefly in a small white bungalow that Gladys had bought after years of scrimping and saving, but their time together was brief. Gladys was plagued by mental illness and spent the rest of her life in and out of institutions, unable to care for Norma Jeane.

At 16, to escape life in an orphanage, Norma Jeane married Jim Dougherty. By 20, she was divorced and on her way to Hollywood… and stardom. Norma Jeane became Marilyn Monroe, one of the world's glamourous movie stars, but deep inside she was still Norma Jeane, a tortured soul who only wanted to be loved. She sought solace in sleeping pills and champagne, but the combination was deadly. On 5 August 1962, Marilyn Monroe was found dead of a drug overdose. Whether her death was an accident or a suicide will never be known. She died alone, still seeking the love and security she had been denied as a child.

Facing page: Innocent yet sensuous, vulnerable yet strong, Marilyn Monroe had a unique magic that will live on forever.

Left: Marilyn, wearing only an enigmatic smile. This photo was taken only a few short months before her death.

Growing Up

Left: Marilyn Monroe was born Norma Jeane Mortensen on 1 June 1926. Norma Jeane spent her early years in a number of foster homes, seeing her mother, Gladys, only on weekends. *Above:* Norma Jeane and Gladys spend the day at the beach.

Left, below: Norma Jeane and her half-sister Bernice. Bernice was the daughter of Gladys and her first husband, Jack Baker. By the time the two women finally met, Bernice was married and living in Florida.

Right, above: On 19 June 1942, Norma Jeane Mortensen married Jim Dougherty. She had just turned 16. Jim soon joined the Merchant Marines, and the two lived on Catalina Island *(right, below)* for a short time. Norma Jeane divorced Jim in 1946 so that she could pursue a career in Hollywood. The photo on the *far right* shows Norma Jeane at Twentieth Century-Fox shortly after she signed her first contract in 1946.

Marilyn, the Model

Above: Norma Jeane began her career as a model at the Blue Book Modeling Agency, headed by Miss Emmilene Snively, who persuaded Norma Jeane to straighten and lighten her hair and to enroll in a modeling course.

Left and right: Rare photographs of promotional work that Norma Jeane did for McDonnell Douglas in 1946.

The Road to Hollywood

Marilyn's career was launched when Army photographer David Conover spotted her at an aircraft factory and picked her for a feature on women doing essential work for the war effort. One of his photos of her appeared on the cover of *Yank* magazine *(right)*.

Above: Marilyn's first movie role was in *Scudda Hoo! Scudda Hay!* (1948). She had one line—but it ended up on the cutting room floor. *Left:* With Groucho Marx, on the set of *Love Happy* (1949).

Glamour Girl

These pages: Glamour shots from the late 1940s and early 1950s. She was beautiful, but Hollywood wasn't satisfied with Norma Jeane. She was renamed Marilyn Monroe and underwent plastic surgery to 'correct' her nose and chin.

There were plenty of glamourous publicity shots, but only a couple of bit parts and Fox soon dropped Marilyn. Undaunted, she spent every cent she earned on acting, singing and dancing lessons.

Ingénue

Above: In *A Ticket to Tomahawk* (1950), Marilyn had a bit part as a chorus girl named Clara. *Left:* Her first leading role was in *Ladies of the Chorus* (1948), in which she played the part of a dancer. Although she received favorable reviews, Columbia, like Twenty Century-Fox, did not renew her contract. *Right:* Marilyn, as a bathing beauty.

The Asphalt Jungle

Above: Hollywood agent Johnny Hyde fell in love with Marilyn and wanted to marry her. He knew he didn't have long to live and wanted Marilyn to inherit his fortune. Even though Marilyn refused to marry a man she didn't love, Hyde remained devoted to her and helped her secure her first major role *(right)* in *The Asphalt Jungle* (1950), in which she played the part of Angela, the mistress of a corrupt lawyer (Louis Calhern).

Left: Marilyn's performance in *The Asphalt Jungle* led to rave reviews and a new contract with Twentieth Century-Fox.

Hollywood Starlet

Above: Marilyn as Miss Caswell in the award-winning *All About Eve* (1950). In this scene, escort Addison De Witt (George Sanders) introduces Miss Caswell to the caustic Margo Channing (Bette Davis) and Eve (Anne Baxter).

Right: In *Clash by Night* (1952), Marilyn co-starred with Keith Andes. *Far right:* As Angela in *The Asphalt Jungle* (1950). Marilyn herself felt the final scene of this film–in which she must chose between telling the truth or supporting Calhern's alibi–was among her best work.

Left: By 1952, Marilyn had perfected her sexy pout.

Sex Symbol

Above: Marilyn won the Henrietta Award for the Best Young Box Office Personality of 1951, but it was her décolletage that attracted the most publicity. The press was scandalized and said she would have looked better in a potato sack…. Marilyn *(left)* was happy to comply with the request.

Right: Marilyn shocked the nation when it was discovered that she had earlier posed nude for a calendar.

Gentlemen Prefer Blondes

Left: Marilyn and Jane Russell in *Gentlemen Prefer Blondes* (1953). Her performance as Lorelei Lee—a role that seemed tailor-made for her—earned her much acclaim and *Photoplay*'s Best Actress Award.

Above: Following their success in *Gentlemen Prefer Blondes*, Marilyn and Jane had their hand and footprints enshrined at Grauman's (now Mann's) Chinese Theatre. Marilyn commented that a bust-print of Jane and buttock-print of herself might be more appropriate.

Right: The movie is famous for Marilyn's rendition of *Diamonds Are a Girl's Best Friend. Far right:* Marilyn Monroe and Jane Russell.

Movie Star

Above: How to Marry a Millionaire was Marilyn's third big hit in 1953. On film, her performance is delightful, but director Jean Negulesco was amazed by her lack of self confidence. *Right:* Her co-stars were Lauren Bacall (center) and Betty Grable (left).

Left: She had to endure her share of bit parts and 'fluff' roles, but a retrospective look at Marilyn's career reveals she was an accomplished actress capable of playing serious parts as well as comedy.

On Hollywood's Roller Coaster

Marilyn's career seemed to be flourishing in the mid-1950s. She starred in six films between 1953 and 1955, but some of her roles were trade-offs and did little to advance her career.

Above: She accepted a small part in *No Business Like Show Business* (1954), a dreary musical tribute to Irving Berlin, because the studio promised her *The Seven Year Itch*.

In *River of No Return* (1954), Marilyn played a saloon singer *(left and right)* involved with an ex-criminal. The off-screen action was as melodramatic as the film itself. Director Otto Preminger banned Marilyn's acting coach, Natasha Lytess, from the set and Marilyn retaliated by staging an ankle injury to delay filming.

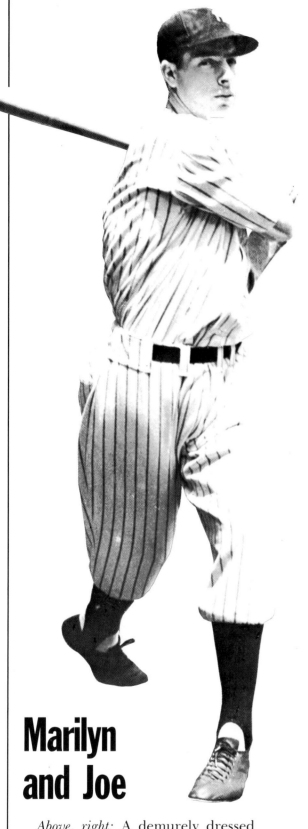

Marilyn and Joe

Above, right: A demurely dressed Marilyn Monroe married baseball legend Joe DiMaggio on 14 January 1951, but Joe objected to Marilyn's *femme fatale* image *(left)* and the marriage lasted only nine months. Despite their differences, Joe remained a loyal friend and escorted Marilyn to the premiere of *The Seven Year Itch* (1955) after their divorce.

Entertaining the Troops

These pages: Marilyn interrupted her honeymoon with Joe DiMaggio to perform for the troops in Korea, in February 1954. The top level brass was afraid Marilyn would incite a riot with the song *Do It Again* and ordered that the words be changed to *Kiss Me Again*. Much to her new husband's dismay, Marilyn thoroughly enjoyed herself and described the tour as 'the highlight of my life.'

The Seven Year Itch

In *The Seven Year Itch* (1955), Marilyn plays the girl upstairs–a model and 'actress' in commercials. Innocent but seductive, she becomes the subject of co-star Tom Ewell's fantasies. In the still *at right*, Marilyn's toe becomes stuck in the bath tub. *Above:* The famous skirt blowing scene, perhaps the most famous scene from all of Marilyn's movies.

Left: A publicity shot from Twentieth Century-Fox.

Marilyn–
At Her Best

Right: This 1953 shot shows Marilyn at her most sensual. *Above:* In 1955, she had a brief affair with Marlon Brando. Lee Strasberg, head of the Actors Studio, characterized the two of them as the greatest raw talents he had ever worked with.

Right: Marilyn's most acclaimed role was as Cherie, the saloon singer in *Bus Stop* (1956).

Egghead Weds Hourglass

In an effort to find meaning in her life, Marilyn married playwright Arthur Miller *(left)* on 29 June 1956. 'Egghead Weds Hourglass' read the headlines, for the press could not imagine a more unlikely couple. *Above, left:* The newlyweds.

Shortly after they were married, they left for England to film *The Prince and the Showgirl* (1957) with Sir Laurence Olivier. At the press conference *(above)* announcing the film, the strap of her dress broke, prompting one of the reporters to ask 'How did it feel?'—a sarcastic reference to Marilyn's Method Acting training.

Once again, the pressures of being Marilyn the Movie Star *(right)* would create problems in her marriage.

The Prince and the Showgirl

Left: Marilyn and husband Arthur Miller at the premiere of *The Prince and the Showgirl* on 13 June 1957. *Above:* The Millers are greeted by Laurence Olivier and his wife, Vivien Leigh, who had played the part of the showgirl on the stage. *Right, above and below:* Scenes from the film.

The Many Faces of Marilyn

Left: This shot of Marilyn mugging for the camera provides a striking contrast to the photo *above* that reveals her vulnerable side. By this point in her career, Marilyn was known for creating problems on the set. She had trouble remembering her lines and was always late for filming. Lauren Bacall, who worked with Marilyn in *How To Marry A Millionaire* (1953), attributed Marilyn's chronic lateness to sheer terror–'She couldn't face what she was being called upon to do.'

Right: Marilyn Monroe–the epitome of glamour and beauty.

Overleaf: Marilyn strikes a seductive pose for this publicity shot for *The Prince and the Showgirl* (1957).

Some Like It Hot

Left: With Jack Lemmon, on the set of *Some Like It Hot* (1959). Lemmon and Tony Curtis played two men on the run from the from the mob who disguise themselves as women and join an all-girl band called Sweet Sue's Society Syncopaters *(right)*. *Left, below:* Marilyn with Tony Curtis (left) and George Raft (right) at a party celebrating the start of filming. Their happy expressions would turn sour as the weeks progressed because of Marilyn's unprofessional behavior. Curtis, in particular, was frustrated by Marilyn's endless retakes. Marilyn had grown increasingly dependent on drugs and alcohol–the end result being that she stumbled through most of the filming.

In spite of the many difficulties surrounding the filming of *Some Like It Hot*, the finished product was highly successful, with Marilyn receiving much acclaim as a comedienne. Her troubles would continue, however. The day after filming ended she suffered a miscarriage.

Right: Marilyn and Jack Lemmon frolic on the beach.

Let's Make Love

Above and right: After her success in *Some Like It Hot*, Marilyn starred with Yves Montand in what turned out to be a dismal failure–*Let's Make Love* (1960).

The film's one saving grace was Marilyn's show-stopping version of Cole Porter's *My Heart Belongs to Daddy*.

The film's failure added to Marilyn's personal heartache. Her marriage to Arthur Miller would soon end in divorce, and her ill-fated affair with co-star Yves Montand added insult to injury when she discovered that Montand had never intended to leave his wife, actress Simone Signoret.

Left: In contrast to her sporadic film career, Marilyn was always at her best when it was just her and the camera, as illustrated by this captivating photo by Philippe Halsman.

Blonde Bombshell

These pages: The ultimate blonde bombshell. She was every man's dream and what every woman dreamed of being. It wasn't until after her death that the public began to see her in a different light and realize that Marilyn had been a victim of her own fame.

The Misfits

Left and above: Marilyn and Clark Gable in *The Misfits* (1961).

Marilyn was eager to appear with Gable. As an adult and an actress, Marilyn admired him, and as a child she had associated him with the man she believed to be her father, for the two men looked remarkably alike.

The Misfits was the final film for both Gable and Marilyn. Gable died of a heart attack two weeks after filming, and although Marilyn would begin another film, she would never complete it.

Right: Marilyn played Roslyn, a vulnerable, newly divorced woman. Written expressly for her by her husband Arthur Miller, the part gave Marilyn the opportunity to play a serious, complex character. Sadly, the role came too late in her career. Her dependency on pills and alcohol interfered with her ability to work, and production had to be halted for two weeks while Marilyn was hospitalized following a drug overdose.

The Tragic Decline of Marilyn

Above: Beneath the facade of Movie Star, Marilyn's pain is reflected in her face. By this time she was addicted to tranquilizers, which she washed down with champagne. *Right:* The burden of maintaining the image of glamour queen *(left)* contributed to Marilyn's physical collapse and, ultimately, to her death in 1962.

Something's Got to Give

Above: Marilyn's final role was in *Something's Got to Give*. She attended only 12 out of 35 days of shooting and her repeated absences from the set led Fox to fire her. After she was fired she told a magazine writer, 'My work is the only ground I've ever had to stand on. To put it bluntly, I seem to be a whole superstructure with no foundation. But I'm working on the foundation.'

Right: On one occasion, Marilyn skipped filming to sing *Happy Birthday* to President John F Kennedy.

Left: Stills of the nude swimming scene from *Something's Got to Give* were published after her death and created a furor to rival that of the famous nude calender.

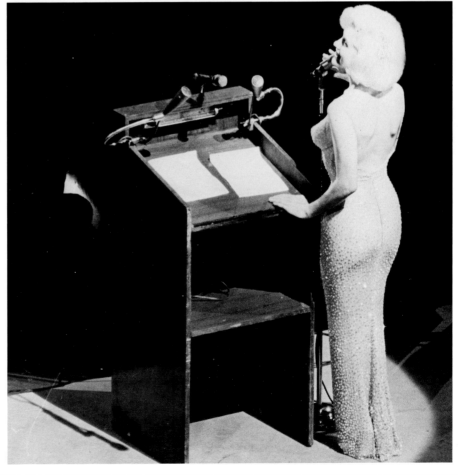

MARILYN MONROE

1926 — 1962

Tributes to Marilyn

Left: Marilyn Monroe's wall crypt at Westwood Memorial Park. For 20 years, Joe DiMaggio had six red roses placed on Marilyn's crypt three times a week.

Right: Her hand and footprints at Grauman's (now Mann's) Chinese Theatre and her star on Hollywood Boulevard *(above)*. Though she was never able to find the love and appreciation she needed in life, Marilyn—and Norma Jeane—will never be forgotten.

Marilyn Remembered

... from her early days at Fox (*above*); as the myopic manhunter in *How to Marry a Millionaire* (*far left*); as the ultimate showgirl (*left*); and as the exuberant leader of the parade.

Overleaf: Marilyn in a publicity shot for *Let's Make Love*.

INDEX

All About Eve 21
Andes, Keith 21
Asphalt Jungle, The 18-19, 21
Bacall, Lauren 27
Baker, Berniece 8
Baxter, Anne 21
Blue Book Modeling Agency 11
Brando, Marlon 36
Bus Stop 36
Calhern, Louis 18
Clash by Night 21
Columbia Pictures 16
Conover, David 12
Curtis, Tony 46-47
Diamonds Are a Girl's Best Friend 25
DiMaggio, Joe 31, 32, 53, 58
Do It Again 32
Dougherty, Jim 6, 8-9
Ewell, Tom 35
Fox *see* Twentieth Century-Fox
Gable, Clark 6, 52-53
Gentlemen Prefer Blondes 24-25
Gifford, Stanley C 6
Grable, Betty 27
Grauman's Chinese Theatre 25, 59
Halsman, Philippe 5, 49
Henrietta Award 22
How to Marry a Millionaire 27, 60
Hyde, Johnny 18
Kennedy, President John F 75
Ladies of the Chorus 16
Leigh, Vivien 41
Lemmon, Jack 46-47

Let's Make Love 49, 60
Love Happy 12
Lytess, Natasha 28
McDonnell Douglas 11
Marx, Groucho 12
Miller, Arthur 38, 40-41, 49, 53
Misfits, The 53
Montand, Yves 49
Mortensen, Edward 6
Mortensen, Gladys 6, 8
My Heart Belongs to Daddy 49
No Business Like Show Business 28
Olivier, Laurence 38, 41
Preminger, Otto 28
Prince and the Showgirl, The 38, 41
Raft, George 46
River of No Return 28-29
Russell, Jane 24-25
Sanders, George 21
Scudda Hoo! Scudda Hay! 12
Seven Year Itch, The 28, 31, 35
Signoret, Simone 51
Snively, Emmilene 11
Some Like It Hot 46-47, 49
Something's Got to Give 56-57
Strasberg, Lee 36
Ticket to Tomahawk, A 16
Twentieth Century-Fox 8, 15, 16, 18, 57, 60
Westwood Memorial Park 59
Widmark, Richard 4
Yank magazine 12

Photo Credits

All photos courtesy of American Graphic Systems Archives except those listed below:
Academy of Motion Picture Arts and Sciences 1, 12 (top), 49 (bottom), 53 (bottom)
Brompton Picture Archives 16 (bottom), 25 (bottom left, right)
© RE DeJauregui 58, 59 (all)
George Zeno Collection 7, 8 (all), 11 (top), 12 (bottom), 14, 15 (left), 17, 18 (top), 21 (bottom right), 22 (right), 23, 25 (top), 30, 31 (top right, bottom), 33, 36 (all), 37, 38 (top left, bottom), 41 (top left), 44-45, 46 (bottom), 48, 57 (bottom), 61, 62-63
Joel Finler Collection 15 (right), 20, 24, 35 (bottom), 38 (top right), 41 (top right, bottom), 46 (top)
McDonnell Douglas 10, 11 (bottom)
National Archives 32 (all)
The National Baseball Hall of Fame and Museum, Inc 31 (top left)
National Film Archives, London 4, 16, (top), 21 (top, bottom left), 27 (all), 29, 40, 47 (all), 49 (top), 52, 54 (bottom), 60 (top, bottom left)
Bob Willoughby 57 (top)